# The Complete and Simple Guide to Challah:

# A Farm Boy's Guide to Great Jewish (and non-Jewish) Breads

Dr. Dean Richards

Dr. Dean Richards

I'd like to dedicate this book of challah recipes to whomever it is who first realized that growing fungus in your bread dough prior to baking it was a good thing (In contrast to growing fungus in your bread after you've baked it, which is decidedly a bad thing.) As whoever first realized that fungus and bread dough go together is lost in antiquity, I dedicate this book to my late mother, who taught me to bake, my wife's family, who gave me my first challah recipe and were kind enough to praise the results, and my wife and children, who unfailingly eat the challah I bake.

Copyright © 2015 by Dr. Dean Richards
All rights reserved.

ISBN-10: 1507681097
ISBN-13: 978-1907681091

# CONTENTS

| | |
|---|---|
| A Few Words about Bread | 5 |
| Braids and Braiding | 16 |
| Hungarian Challah (Rotholtz Recipe) | 26 |
| Traditional Challah | 29 |
| Traditional Challah for Sandwiches | 32 |
| Apple Cinnamon Challah | 35 |
| Cinnamon Sugar Challah | 39 |
| Challah with Chocolate Tunnels | 43 |
| Caramelized Onion Challah | 46 |
| Caramelized Onion Challah with Parmesean | 49 |
| Jalapeño Cheese Challah | 52 |
| Garlic and Herb Challah | 55 |
| Challah with Raisins or Craisins | 58 |
| Garlic Lover's Challah | 61 |
| Cheese Challah | 64 |
| Salted Chocolate Challah | 67 |
| Pesto Challah | 70 |
| Traditional Croissants | 73 |
| Pita | 84 |
| Farm-House Cinnamon Rolls | 86 |
| Onion Bialys | 90 |

Dr. Dean Richards

# A Few Words About Bread (and why I'm qualified to speak those words)

Let me open this guide to one of Judaism's greatest contributions to cuisine by admitting that I am not, myself, Jewish. I'm an Iowa farm boy, having grown up on a dairy farm in Southeastern Iowa. Throughout my childhood we milked cows, every morning and every night of every day, and we tended the calves that would eventually become the next generation of cows (or the tasty steaks and hamburger dishes on our table and the tables of others). We also baled mountains of hay to feed said cows through the winter and raised and harvested cribs full of corn to feed stock and to sell for cash, and we spent inordinate amounts of time removing very large piles of manure from barns and barnyards, the inevitable end result of feeding all those animals. So how does a former farm boy end up writing a recipe book about challah?

No, not from my mother. My mother wasn't big on baking bread. In her opinion, prepared, packaged, store-bought, sliced bread was the best thing since, well, sliced bread. It isn't that she didn't cook and didn't enjoy baking—she was the queen of cookies and pies, and the things she could do with choice cuts of beef or plain, mundane hamburger and an oven or stove were phenomenal. But now and then she would make home-made doughnuts or cinnamon rolls, and those days were magical. For one thing, she didn't believe in half-measures. She had three large, healthy sons and a husband, all of whom engaged in the necessary heavy physical activity of farm work in the mid 20$^{th}$ century and all of whom had prodigious appetites. On the days she decided to make cinnamon rolls, the quantity of dough that would be rising during the day was impressive to start with, and as it rose, it became truly phenomenal. Later in the day, that dough would be rolled out into large slabs, be covered liberally with butter, cinnamon, and sugar, and then be rolled into spirals that quickly rose to fill huge pans. By supper time (we were farm folk—the midday meal was dinner, and the last meal of the day was supper—there was no such thing as "lunch" in our house) the pans, now brimming with cinnamon-sugar goodness, would slide into the oven and fill the room with the unparalleled and absolutely heavenly smell of baking bread and hot cinnamon and sugar.

Sometime after I hit double digits in age, I decided I wanted to know how to make cinnamon rolls, and my mother, undoubtedly starved for a daughter to teach her many culinary skills, was more than happy to initiate me into the tricks of proofing yeast, judging when flour quantities were just right, and knowing when to add more water to get just the right dough appearance. By the time I drifted off to college and then graduate school, I could make passable cinnamon rolls and raised doughnuts, and I'd collected several decent bread recipes I could trot out for the occasional potluck or holiday dinner.

But I managed to get to my mid-20's without having even heard the word "challah," let alone thought about baking any. Part of the reason for this is that there were no Jewish people where I grew up. None. Zero. No Jewish people attended our local community school, nor did we have any Jewish teachers or administrators. I knew nothing of the sheer culinary simplicity of lox, ripe tomato, and red onion on a bagel, or the incredible decadence of latkes and brisket. I'd never had kreplach or kugel, and the first time I saw matzo was in the college cafeteria during Passover. Of the elegant, braided, golden airiness of challah I was completely ignorant.

So what happened that has led to me claiming enough expertise on the central item of the Shabbat table to feel confident enough to write a recipe book on the subject? The most likely and obvious thing, of course--I married a Jewish girl. Actually, that's an understatement that doesn't really do the event justice, so I'll elaborate: I married the loveliest and most intelligent young single woman I'd ever met, and she happened to be Jewish. I was welcomed with open arms into her large and close family, and then my wife and I added three more children to that family group, and her sister and brother-in-law added 4 more, and we became quite a large group at family gatherings.

These family gatherings then provided the next step along the way of my challah adventure. I started bringing various breads to holiday gatherings, and those breads were received in a most gratifying fashion. And then one day my wife's mother, Helene (and don't you dare to call her Helen), mentioned that she had an old family recipe for challah, that no one had made lately because they "really weren't bread bakers," but maybe I would want to give it a try. The recipe card itself actually described the bread as "cholla," and its origin is as charming a story as its misspelled name. This recipe had originated from my wife's great-grandmother, who grew up in Germany. But the recipe itself isn't German. As the story was related to me, this lady, whose name was Licien Rotholtz, grew up in an upper-middle class household full of servants to do the dirty work that the ladies of the household preferred not to do, including Hungarian cooks to bake the bread. Young Licien was fascinated by the cooks and their efforts, and spent many hours hanging around the kitchen, watching and then eventually helping prepare the household dishes. As was the case with many people of that era, she learned to cook by eyeballing quantities, throwing in this and that ingredient until the amount looked right and never measuring anything. When she emigrated to America with the family in the early 1900s, the kitchen became her domain and she prepared most of the family dishes until deep into old age. At that point it suddenly dawned on my wife's mother and her sister Janet that the recipe for the challah they knew and loved so well existed only in this dear old lady's head and might someday be lost for good. So one morning Janet sat down with her grandmother as she prepared challah, and then stopped her as she added each ingredient so that she could measure the quantities of each and note them down for posterity. I'm told it went something like this: "There, that's about the right amount of flour. Now you add the sugar..." "Wait a minute, let me measure the flour..." (Patient sigh while frantic measuring occurs.) "Now you add the sugar...." "Wait a minute—how much sugar?!! Don't throw it in yet, I need to measure it..." (More patient sighing while more frantic measuring occurs...).

Anyway, in the end there was this recipe, dutifully noted on a card, and no one had made it in quite some time. I looked at it and said, well, bread is bread, right? I might as well give it a go. That's how my challah adventures began. The Rotholtz recipe turned out excellent—a heavier but very sweet challah perfect for holidays like Thanksgiving or Hanukkah. I added the recipe to my other bread recipes, but for a long time when I said I was making challah, this was the bread I was making. In fact, it's the first recipe in this collection, listed under "Hungarian Challah (Rotholtz Family Recipe)".  Then the final piece fell into place that led to where we are today, with the production of this challah recipe collection.  My children grew up.

Actually that last event took what seemed to be a very long time, but that also seemed to have passed in a moment.  There was a house full of small children who had to be chivvied through chores and piano practice and helped with homework and read bedtime stories, then there were these three young adults headed off to colleges.  A lot happened in between, but a much of it is now just a blur in my mind.  Our oldest son headed off to pursue a doctorate in chemical engineering and moved to Seattle.  Our daughter's talent in art unfolded and off she went across the country to Rhode Island to pursue her studies at their very fine (and very expensive) School of Design.  And our middle child and second son realized that his calling was to attend rabbinical school and become a rabbi.

Up until that point, I'd made challah when the urge hit me, or when there was a family gathering, or when a holiday called for it.  Suddenly, I had a practicing rabbinical student in the house, a rabbinical student who needed a fresh challah (actually, two fresh challahs) every Friday evening for Shabbat.  I found myself baking challah every week, and quickly tired of the same recipe over and over again.  I started seeking out new recipes to try, challahs that were very different from each other so that I could avoid the same old routine.  Also, because some meals were meat meals and some were dairy, I also needed corresponding recipes so I could match up to the meals we were having Friday nights.  My sister-in-law and other family members started looking out for recipes for me and sending them by, and I started experimenting with various ones, invariably changing them as I did. I simplified some recipe steps that did not seem to be necessary for the quality of the outcome, altered ingredient balances to be more to our tastes, and tried different added ingredients to give special flavors. Pretty soon I had a stack of altered, annotated, stained, and ragged pages that I would find myself flipping through, trying to decide what to make for a particular week. My wife 3-hole punched the pages and put them in a binder that I kept in the kitchen cabinets.  But the recipes themselves were a mess, and I found myself thinking one day that I should go through and correct them on the computer, making new, legible, and more accurate copies. That's when it occurred to me that I really should put the whole mess together, along with all I've learned about bread baking over the years, and then publish them on Amazon.  It was a process I was already was familiar with, because several years ago I published two books for lay people on the subject of psychology, **Psychology in Plain English**, and **More Psychology in Plain English**, and both books have sold well and garnered some very gratifying reviews.  (I'm a professor of psychology when I'm not baking bread).  So I determined that during the next university break I'd gather my challah recipes and put them together with a few other favored bread recipes.  I also decided to make the recipe book one that accomplished cooks can simply dive into, but also one that people who have never baked bread before can follow with confidence and, hopefully, good results.

Which is how we got to where we are now.  If you're new to bread baking, you might want to read the general tips on bread baking, bread braiding, and baking equipment first before diving into the recipes. If you're an old hand at this, just skip right to the recipes themselves.  Years ago, my mother used to listen religiously to a regional radio program known as "Kitchen Klatter." The program was produced by a family in Western Iowa, and every program involved a recipe or two that had been passed along through their family's generations or the generations of other families. The most positive thing about the program is that you could count on their recipes—if they broadcast a recipe over the radio, it had been tested, personally, by them, and only when they were sure they liked it did they pass it along. This recipe book follows that pattern--every recipe in this book has been tested on my extended family and friends, and I stand by every single one of them. I simply hope you'll enjoy them as much as we have. Now, on to the bread baking!

## A word about serious bread-baking...

It's possible to bake wonderful bread with virtually no equipment at all. Our ancestors threw flour, yeast (or bread starter that continuously fermented on a windowsill), sugar, and water on a board and kneaded the whole mess together by hand, covered it with a cloth to let it rise, kneaded it again, and then split it into portions and baked it in a wood-fired oven. They didn't use pans, mixing bowls, measuring cups and spoons, or precise, temperature-controlled ovens, and I'm told they made very good bread that way. But there are a number of things that can make bread-making much easier and quicker, and some things the average person who hasn't made bread before might find useful, so I'd like to turn to those items before proceeding. Expert bread bakers can simply skip this part.

First, I'd recommend if you're going to make bread often to get a serious mixer, such as the large Kitchen-Aid or Cuisinart models that handle 5 or 7-quart bowls. Such a mixer comes with a large dough hook that's perfect for making bread, and has enough power to knead the bread for you all the way through the final stages. These mixers can easily handle the dough for 2 large loaves in one batch, and completely eliminate the need for hand kneading. Frankly, if I had to hand-knead bread I'd probably still make it, but a high-quality large mixer makes the preparation process a snap. If you have a smaller mixer with a dough hook you can use it as well, but I'd cut each recipe in half and mix each half individually if using a smaller mixer so as not to overwhelm the machine. You probably will also have to do the final kneading by hand with a smaller mixer as well.

I'd also recommend you get a large plastic breadboard for rolling out breads, preferably one at least 2 feet square (60 cm X 60 cm). This makes both preparation and cleanup a snap, and gives you a nice, flat, clear surface to work on. You need a good rolling pin, of course, a sharp knife, and a pastry brush now and then for spreading butter or for brushing the tops of the challah with egg. Beyond that, there is not much in the way of specialty equipment one needs to make really excellent bread.

Next, there's the issue of flour. You generally have three choices in white flour—cake flour, all purpose flour, and bread flour. Cake flour has a lower protein content, and thus is used in recipes where you want a smooth, flaky consistency to the product. All purpose flour has more protein than cake flour. Those proteins join together when the bread is worked by mixing or kneading, forming a substance known as gluten. Gluten makes dough elastic and helps it hold together after baking, even when sliced quite thinly. Bread flour has somewhat more protein in it than all purpose flour, and thus helps the bread develop slightly more gluten during the mixing and kneading process. Bread made with bread flour can be counted on to hold together better after baking, and to develop a chewier texture, which may be better for thin slicing, such as making sandwiches. But for making challah, all purpose flour is perfectly fine suitable and will create fine results.

Then there's the issue of salt. Many people are on a reduced salt diet and wonder about the quantities of salt used in bread recipes. But it's not wise to eliminate salt from bread recipes. For one thing, the resulting taste of the bread will be greatly diminished without the salt. (I once forgot to include the salt in a challah recipe I was making. I realized my mistake as soon as I bit into it—it was dull, flavorless, and, frankly, tasted like it needed salt).

The other purpose salt serves in bread recipes is in aiding gluten development and in inhibiting the growth of bacteria that might weaken the gluten in bread as it rises. The combination of these two things help the bread develop a finer texture and hold it together while rising as well as when it's cut after baking.

You may notice that in all the recipes I have in this book the salt is not added until after some flour has been mixed into the recipe. This is because if you added the salt directly to the yeast mixture before adding the flour, the salinity of the yeast mixture might become so great that many of the yeast cells you just went through all that work to start would be destroyed, and that will slow the rising of your bread. If you wait to add salt until after some of the flour is mixed in, the salt content doesn't rise so high and the yeast isn't disturbed nearly as much.

Finally, there's the issue of the amount of water you need to use for the amount of flour you're using. Flour varies in water content, so some flours on some days absorb less water, and other flours on other days will need more. Most bread bakers deal with this variability by using a set amount of water, but varying the amount of flour used in the recipe from one time to the next. That's why most bread recipes provide approximate amounts when it comes to flour, for example, "5-7 cups flour." There's simply no way of knowing how much flour you'll need for that recipe on a given day. So how do you know how much flour to add to your liquid ingredients? The easiest thing to do is to combine all the other ingredients with about 3 cups of flour and thoroughly mix that, and then gradually add in flour about half a cup at a time until the dough reaches the right consistency. You'll know you've added enough flour when the dough loses almost all of its stickiness and can be molded by hand into a smooth, elastic ball. It's best to start with the dough too wet and then slowly add the flour until it reaches the proper, drier consistency, because if you add too much flour all at once and make the dough too dry, it's very hard to work more water into the dough at that point.

## The Origins of Challah and the Word "Challah"

If you're wondering about the origins of modern day challah, most food historians agree that the fluffy, braided white bread we call challah arose in the Southern section of Germany sometime during the Middle Ages. At the time, it would have been a welcome Shabbat departure from the rougher, whole grain bread that was usually eaten on other days. As the custom in Southern Germany at the time was to braid special, holiday breads into decorative shapes, challah was also braided. As Jewish populations spread from there into Poland, Russia, and Eastern

Europe, this bread went with them and became the traditional Shabbat treat.

But the word "challah" has a different and much older origin. Biblical references in *Numbers* and in *Leviticus* talk about the portion of dough that should be set aside as a sacrifice when baking. That portion is referred to as the "hallah" and translates roughly into "that which is separated." The first apparent reference to Shabbat bread by that same term doesn't occur until the 15th century in a German work of *Halacha* entitled the *Leket Yosher*. In that work, families were instructed to prepare two breads for the Shabbat, and those breads were referred to as "hallah" in that passage. That usage of the word became common, morphing into the modern word "challah." (You see, you learn a thing or two by having a rabbinical student in the house.)

Traditionalists harkening back to that instruction often prepare two challahs for Shabbat, probably in honor of the two portions of manna that the Israelites were given on Shabbat during the exodus. Some bakers strive to create 12 humps in their braid, to correspond to the 12 tribes of Israel. And challahs baked for the Jewish New Year are traditionally round, signifying the continuity of life from one year to the next, as well as containing added sugar for a sweet new year.

# Braids and Braiding

The traditional way of preparing challah is to braid the dough. This not only makes the breads look much more fancy and elegant, but it serves a practical purpose. For millennia, when families would gather around the candles on Shabbat and recite the blessing of the bread, the leader would then distribute the now blessed bread to the others present by pulling off chunks and handing them about. Braided bread is ideal for dismembering and distributing in this fashion, as it separates easily into nicely-sized portions without protest. (And nobody wants protesting challah.)

But, although challah was traditionally braided, there are many different challah braids. There are three-, four-, five-, and six-strand braids, knotted braids, round braids, and spiral braids, Mogen David (Star of David) braids and even braids that look like a bunch of grapes. Each has its own distinctive appearance, and each is elegant and practical. I'm not going to document all the ways to braid challah here, but will confine myself to the simpler and more practical braids, leaving it up to the reader to research other braids, if desired, through the Internet or other sources. Mainly, I'll be focusing on two very useful braids—the 3 strand rectangular challah braid, and the 4-strand round challah braid. For traditionalists, they also have an advantage that some other braids don't have. Once braided and baked, a 3-strand rectangular challah usually has 6 humps in its top, so a pair of them, the double helping of dough that is mandated for Shabbat, has twelve humps. A large, double-sized 4-strand round challah also has twelve humps on the top once braided and baked.

## The Three-Strand Rectangular Braid

The three-strand rectangular braid is perhaps the simplest of all challah braids. You simply start with three snakes of dough roughly 24" (60 cm) long, and lay them side-by-side with a space between each of them to give you room to braid. (Here's a challah baker's tip—if one of your three strands is larger than the others, start with it as the center rope—it just works better that way). You begin by pinching the three strands together at one end, then tuck the pinched part under the end of the loaf.

Then starting with the strand on the right, you bring the outside strand to the middle, across the strand that was previously the middle strand. The right strand will now be in the middle position, and the middle strand will be on the right.

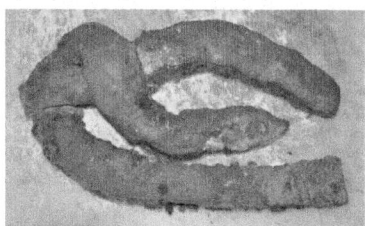

Next, you bring the outside strand on the left across the strand that is now in the middle, making it the middle strand.

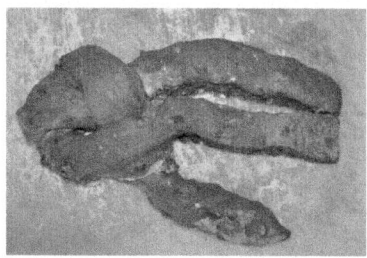

Thereafter, you repeat that process over and over, bringing first the right strand to the middle and then the left, until you get to the end of the strands.

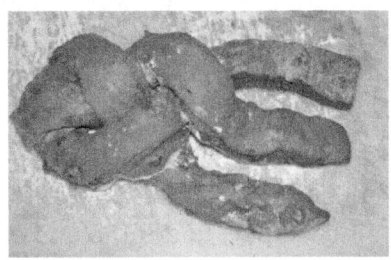

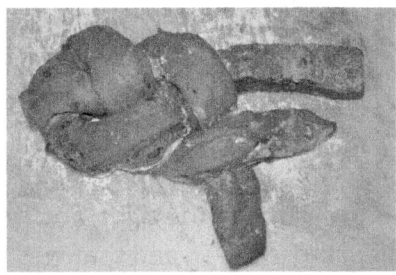

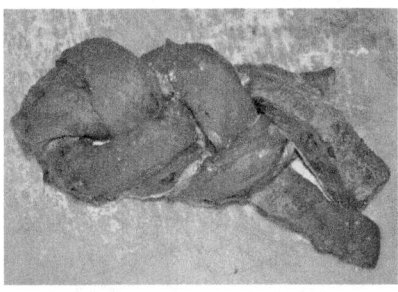

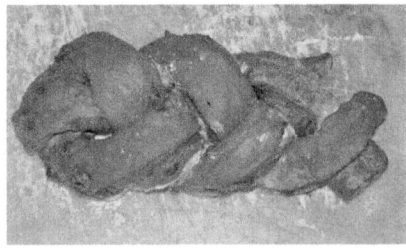

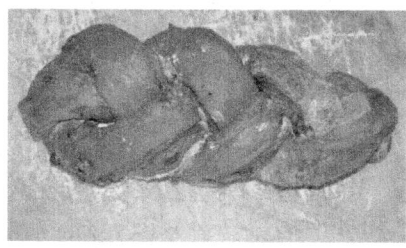

At that point, pinch the ends of the dough together, and tuck the pinched end under the loaf.

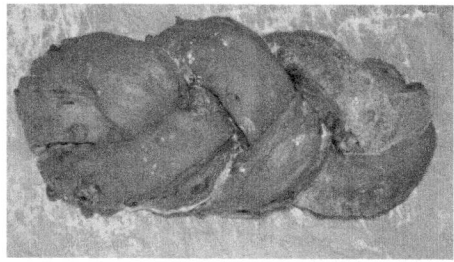

After baking, it looks something like this:

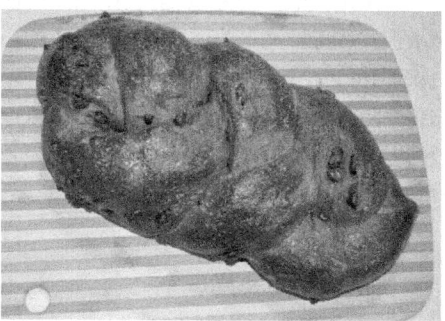

## The Four-Strand Round Braid

The four-strand round braid is just as simple.  Start  with 4 snakes of dough roughly 24" long.  Lay two of them side-by-side right next to each other.  Then lay the other two across the first two, weaving them between the first two like you would if you were weaving a basket.  Your top strand will be over the left vertical strand and under the right, and your bottom strand will be under the left vertical strand and over the right, as shown below.

Now on each side of your "basket" you'll have two strands extending outward, one with a strand of bread running over it from the other direction, and one with a strand running under it.  Starting with the leftmost strand at the 12 o'clock position, take that strand and turn it across the strand to its left, so that it now points out the side.  Repeat that process on the other three sides of the loaf.  Once you're done your bread will look like this:

Now, you'll have a long and a short strand pointing toward each of the clock positions of 12 o'clock, 3 o'clock, 6 o'clock, and 9 o'clock.  The long strand on each side will have another strand going over it, and the short strand on each side will have another strand going under it. Starting at 12 o'clock, take the long strand that has another passing over it and fold it across the short strand that points to the same clock position on that side. Do this for all four sides again. Your end result will look like this:

Now you can just tuck the remaining ends under the loaf, and your round challah is ready for baking.

After baking, it looks something like this:

## The Four-Strand Rectangular Braid

The four-strand rectangular braid really isn't all that complicated, either. You start with four somewhat thinner snakes of dough roughly 24" (60 cm) long, and lay them side-by-side with a space between each of them wider than the width of the braids.

As with three-strand challah, you begin by pinching the four strands together at one end.

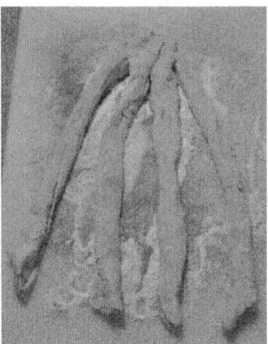

Then starting with the strand on the right, you weave it through the others, going over the first, under the second, and over the third so it becomes the strand that is on the left.

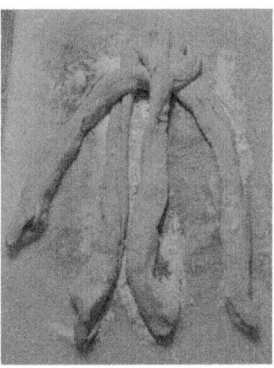

Now you repeat that process, bringing the strand that is now on the right over the first strand to the left, under the second, and over the third.

You simply keep doing this until you get to the end of the strands. At that point, pinch the ends of the dough together, and tuck the pinched end under the loaf. Return to the top and tuck that pinched end under the loaf to complete the process. After baking, it looks something like this:

## The Three-Strand, Double Braid

For this one, you start by cutting about 1/5 of the dough off the rest and putting it aside. The remaining piece is then made into three strands about 24" (50 cm) long. Those you weave together using the three-strand, rectangular braid. Then take the small piece you put aside and weave it into a very small, three-strand rectangular braid and rest it on top of the larger braid.

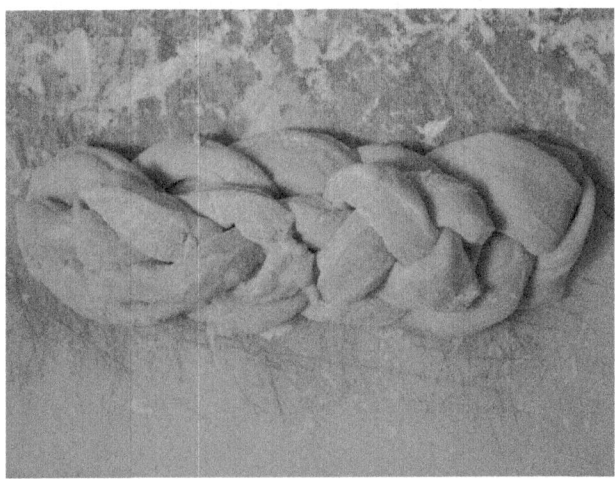

After baking, it looks something like this:

## Spiral Braiding

This one is nearly mindless. To make the spiral or turban challah braid, you simply make your entire dough recipe into a very long snake. Both ends should gradually thin until they come to a point. Starting in the center, tuck that point in tightly and roll the strand around it in a spiral until you get to the other end of the strand. Tuck the second pointed end under the loaf and the turban or spiral braid is complete.

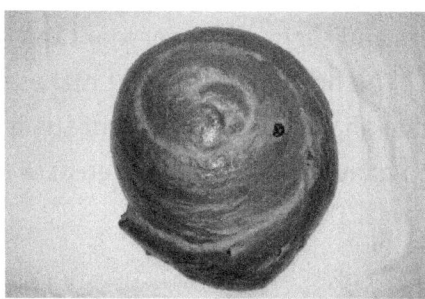

## Knotted Challah

Okay, this one is even easier. Make your dough into one long strand. Pick up the two ends and tie a loose knot in the dough. Bring the loose ends together and pinch them to complete the knot. Place the knot on a baking sheet with the pinched together seam on the bottom so that it's hidden from sight.

# Hungarian Challah, Rotholz Family Recipe (Pareve)

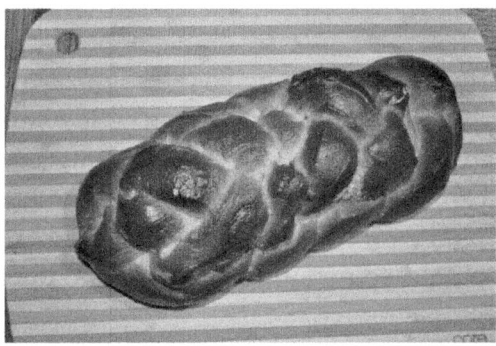

This is a very sweet and slightly heavier loaf than traditional European challah. The high sugar content makes the crust darker than traditional challah, with a hint of burnt sugar. It's great for holiday meals, and a favorite of the children as well as the adults in our family.

**Yeast preparation:**

½ cup water (120 ml) (110 degrees or 40 degrees centigrade)
2 packets or 5 tsp of yeast (25 ml)
1 tsp. sugar (5 ml)

Mix the water, sugar and yeast in the mixing bowl. Let sit for a few minutes to make sure the yeast is active and begins foaming, then proceed to dough preparation.

**Dough Preparation:**

1 cup water (225 ml)
1 egg
5-7 cups flour (1125-1575 ml)
2 tsp. salt (10 ml)
1 ¼ cups sugar (280 ml)

Add water, sugar, and egg to yeast mixture, along with 3 cups (675ml) of flour. Mix using dough hooks until batter is smooth. Mix in salt. Gradually add flour, ½ cup (120 ml) at a time, until dough is losing its stickiness, but is still a bit wet and sticky. (Most bread recipes should be elastic and not quite sticky at this point, but this one really needs to do a spongy rising initially because it's a bit heavier than most. So leave the dough a bit wet and sticky through this first rising). Place in an oiled bowl in a warm location and cover with a kitchen towel to keep the dough from drying out. Allow the dough to rise for a minimum of 3 hours, punching it down periodically when it rises to the top of the bowl. After that first rising, add some flour and knead briefly by hand to remove the stickiness prior to braiding .

**Braiding:**

The instructions below are for making one large rectangular challah, but the recipe works perfectly well for 1 large round, 2 small rectangular, or 2 small round challahs. If you prefer that it's easy to alter the number of braids and the way you braid them.

1 large, rectangular challah:

Split dough into 3 equal parts. Using your hands, form each part into a snake about 20-24" (50-60 cm) long . Braid on a greased cookie sheet or jelly roll pan following the braiding instructions for the rectangular, three braid challah. Let dough rise for another 2 hours or so.

**Baking:**

Preheat your oven to 350 degrees (180 C). If you prefer your challahs glossy on the outside, make an egg wash by mixing 1 egg with one tbsp. (15 ml) of cold water.  Brush the egg wash over the outside surface of the challah.  Bake until golden brown on the outside, which can take anywhere from ½ hour to 45minutes, depending on your oven.  You will know it is done when the creases in the braids are browning and the loaf sounds hollow when you knock on it.

# Traditional Challah (Dairy or Pareve)

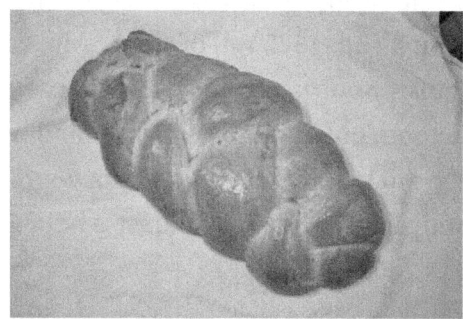

This is a very yellow challah due to the large number of eggs used in it. It's also fairly sweet due to the use of brown sugar along with white sugar. It's a great traditional challah recipe and goes well with a wide variety of foods.

**Yeast preparation:**

½ cup water (120 ml) (110 degrees, or 40 degrees centigrade)
3 packets or 7 1/2 tsp of yeast (38 ml)
1 tsp. sugar (5 ml)

Mix the water, sugar and yeast in the mixing bowl. Let sit for a few minutes to make sure the yeast is active and begins foaming, then proceed to dough preparation.

**Dough Preparation:**

1 1/2 cups water (340 ml)
4 eggs
¼ cup brown sugar (60 ml)
¼ cup white sugar (60 ml)
½ cup of butter (or pareve margarine for pareve challah) (120 ml)
7-8 cups flour (1575-1800 ml)
1 tbsp. salt (15 ml)

Soften the margarine or butter by leaving it out for several hours, or by microwaving it briefly. Add water, sugar, and egg to yeast mixture, along with 3 cups (675 ml) of flour. Mix using dough hooks until batter is smooth. Mix in salt. Gradually add flour, ½ cup (120 ml) at a time, until dough is smooth and not sticky. Cover with a clean kitchen towel and place in a greased bowl in a warm location and allow to rise for at least 3 hours, punching it down periodically.

**Braiding:**

The instructions below are for making one large rectangular challah, but the recipe works perfectly well for 1 large round, 2 small rectangular, or 2 small round challahs. If you prefer that, it's easy to alter the number of braids and the way you braid them. For one large, rectangular challah, split the dough into 3 equal parts. Using your hands, form each part into a snake about 20-24" long (50-60cm). Braid on a greased cookie sheet or jelly roll pan following the braiding instructions for the rectangular, three braid challah. Cover with a clean kitchen towael and let dough rise for another 2 hours or so.

**Baking:**

Preheat your oven to 350 degrees (180 C). If you prefer your challahs glossy on the outside, make an egg wash by mixing 1 egg with one tbsp. (15 ml) of cold water. Brush the egg wash over the outside surface of the challah. Likewise, if you like sesame seeds or poppy seeds on your challah, you can sprinkle a tablespoon of one or the other across the top after brushing with the egg wash.

Bake until the humps of the challah are golden brown and the crevices are starting to brown, and when the challah sounds hollow when you knock on it, which can take anywhere from ½ hour to 45 minutes depending on your oven and the braid you've made.

# Traditional Challah for Sandwiches (Dairy or Pareve)

This is the same as the previous traditional challah recipe with the exception that it is braided into a traditional bread pan, and it leaves out the brown sugar. This makes it less sweet, and thus ideal for sandwiches or children's lunches.

**Yeast preparation:**

½ cup water (120 ml) (110 degrees, or 40 degrees centigrade)
3 packets or 7 1/2 tsp of yeast (38 ml)
1 tsp. sugar (5 ml)

Mix the water, sugar and yeast in the mixing bowl. Let sit for a few minutes to make sure the yeast is active and begins foaming, then proceed to dough preparation.

**Dough Preparation:**

1 1/2 cups water (340 ml)
4 eggs
¼ cup sugar (60 ml)
½ cup of butter (or pareve margarine if making pareve challah) (120 ml)
7-8 cups flour (1575-1800 ml)
1 tbsp. salt (15 ml)

Soften the margarine or butter by leaving it out for several hours, or by microwaving it briefly. Add water, sugar, and egg to yeast mixture, along with 3 cups (675 ml) of flour. Mix using dough hooks until batter is smooth. Mix in salt. Gradually add flour, ½ cup (120 ml) at a time, until dough is smooth and not sticky. Cover with a clean kitchen towel and place in a greased bowl in warm location and allow to rise for at least 3 hours, punching it down periodically.

**Braiding:**

The instructions below are for making 2 sandwich loaves, but the recipe can also be braided into 1 large rectangular challah, 1 large round, 2 small rectangular, or 2 small round challahs. If you prefer that it's easy to alter the number of braids and the way you braid them.

For sandwich bread, split dough into 2 parts, then split each of those into 3 equal parts. Using your hands, form each part into a snake about 20-24" long (50-60cm). Braid 3 of these snakes together on the bread board, then lift the entire braided section into a greased 5" by 9" (13 cm. by 23 cm.) bread pan. Repeat for the second loaf. Cover with a clean kitchen towel and let dough rise for another 2 hours or so.

**Baking:**

Preheat your oven to 350 degrees (180 C). If you prefer your challahs glossy on the outside, make an egg wash by mixing 1 egg with one tbsp. (15 ml) of cold water. Brush the egg wash over the outside surface of the challah.  Likewise, if you like sesame seeds or poppy seeds on your challah, you can sprinkle a tablespoon (15 ml) of one or the other across the top after brushing with the egg wash.  Bake until the humps of the challah are golden brown and the crevices are starting to brown, and when the challah sounds hollow when you knock on it, which can take anywhere from ½ hour to 45 minutes depending on your oven.

# Apple Cinnamon Challah (Pareve)

This is a great challah for Rosh Hashanah due to the apples and honey included in it, but also is just a nice fruit challah for everyday enjoyment.

**Yeast preparation:**

½ cup water (120 ml) (110 degrees, or 40 degrees centigrade)
1 packet or 2 ½ tsp of yeast (13 ml)
1 tsp. sugar (5 ml)

Mix the water, sugar and yeast in the mixing bowl. Let sit for a few minutes to make sure the yeast is active and begins foaming, then proceed to dough preparation.

**Dough Preparation:**

1 cup water (225 ml)
1 egg
3 egg yolks
¾ cup honey (165 ml)
2 tbsp. vegetable oil (30 ml)
5-7 cups flour (1125-1575ml)
2 tsp. salt (10 ml)
2 tsp. vanilla (10 ml)

Add water, egg and egg yolk, honey, and oil to the yeast mixture, along with 3 cups (675 ml) of flour. Mix using dough hooks until batter is smooth. Mix in salt and vanilla. Gradually add flour, ½ cup (120 ml) at a time, until dough is smooth and not sticky. Cover with a clean kitchen towel and place in a greased bowl in warm location and allow to rise for at least 3 hours, punching it down periodically.

**Apple Cinnamon Filling Preparation:**

3 large apples of your favorite baking variety. Granny Smith and Golden Delicious both work well, but any good baking apple will serve fine.

¼ cup sugar (60 ml)
1-2 tbsp. cinnamon (15-30 ml) (more or less, depending on your tastes)
Peel the apples and dice them into ¼ inch (1 cm) cubes, then toss them with the sugar and cinnamon

**Braiding:**

The instructions below are for making two smaller round challahs, but the recipe works perfectly well for 1 large round, 2 small rectangular, or 1 large rectangular challah. If you prefer that it's easy to alter the number of braids and the way you braid them.

For 2 small, round challahs:

Split dough into 2 parts. One at a time, use a rolling pin to roll each half into a rectangle about 20-24" long (50-60 cm.), and 12" wide (30 cm.)

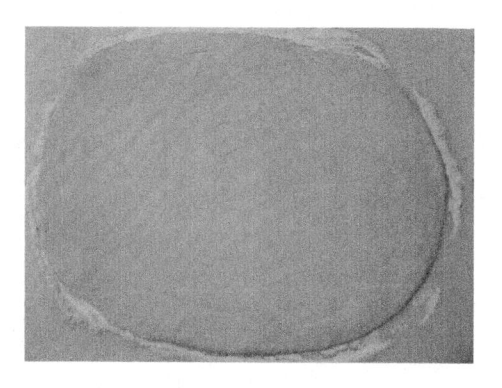

Cut each rectangle into 4 equal parts lengthwise, so you have 4 sections about 20-24" long (50-60 cm.) and 3" wide (8 cm.).

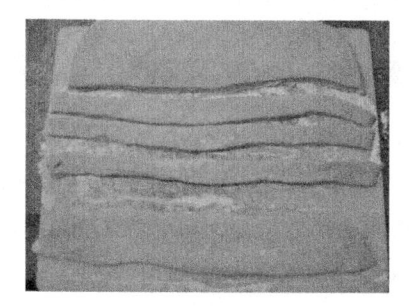

Divide the apples into eight even portions to allow one portion for each of the braids you'll be making. Spread the apples evenly along the center of each snake, then pull the sides of the snake up over the apples and pinch the dough together, creating dough tunnels full of apples.

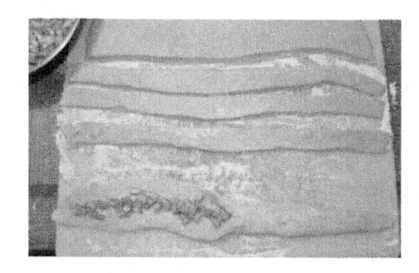

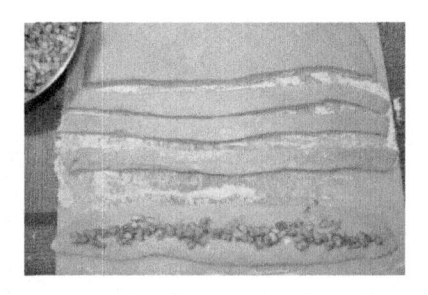

Pinch the ends together as well, sealing the apples in the dough.

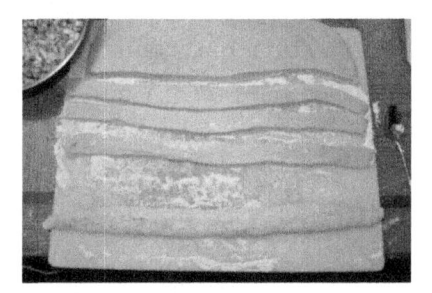

Braid each set of 4 into a round challah onto a greased jelly roll pan or cookie sheet, following the braiding instructions for the 4-strand, round challah braid. Cover with a clean kitchen towel and let dough rise for another 2 hours or so.

**Baking:**

Preheat your oven to 350 degrees (180 cm). If you prefer your challahs glossy on the outside, make an egg wash by mixing 1 egg with one tbsp. (15 ml) of cold water. Brush the egg wash over the outside surface of the challah. Bake until the humps of the challah are golden brown and the crevices are starting to brown, and when the challah sounds hollow when you knock on it, which can take anywhere from ½ hour to 45 minutes depending on your oven.

# Cinnamon Sugar Challah (Dairy or Pareve)

This is more of a dessert or breakfast challah than anything else. It strongly resembles cinnamon rolls in taste and consistency, and makes great breakfast toast as well as the perfect bread for French toast.

**Yeast preparation:**

½ cup water (120 ml) (110 degrees, or 40 degrees centigrade)
1 packet or 2 ½ tsp of yeast (13 ml)
1 tsp. sugar (5 ml)

Mix the water, sugar and yeast in the mixing bowl. Let sit for a few minutes to make sure the yeast is active and begins foaming, then proceed to dough preparation.

**Dough Preparation:**

1 cup water (225 ml)
1 egg
3 egg yolks
¾ cup honey (165 ml)
2 tbsp. vegetable oil (45 ml)
5-7 cups flour (1125-1575 ml)
2 tsp. salt (10 ml)

2 tsp. vanilla (10 ml)

Add water, egg and egg yolk, honey, and oil to the yeast mixture, along with 3 cups (675 ml) of flour. Mix using dough hooks until batter is smooth. Mix in salt and vanilla. Gradually add flour, ½ cup (120 ml) at a time, until dough is smooth and not sticky. Cover with a clean kitchen towel and place in a greased bowl in warm location and allow to rise for at least 3 hours, punching it down periodically.

**Cinnamon-Sugar Application and Braiding:**

1 stick of butter (125 ml) (or 1 stick of pareve margarine if making pareve challah)
Sufficient sugar and cinnamon to cover the rolled-out dough

The instructions below are for making two smaller round challahs, but the recipe works perfectly well for 1 large round, 2 small rectangular, or 1 large rectangular challah. If you prefer that, it's easy to alter the number of braids and the way you braid them.

Soften the butter or margarine (the microwave oven is very handy for this). Split dough into 2 parts. One at a time, use a rolling pin to roll each half into a rectangle about 20-24" long (50-60 cm.), and 12" wide (30 cm.)

Using a pastry brush or spreader, evenly cover the surface with butter or margarine (this will take about half of your butter or margarine, the other half will be used for the second loaf).

Sprinkle sugar liberally over the surface, making an even layer. Sprinkle cinnamon on top of the sugar, covering it evenly as well. Cut the dough lengthwise into 4 equal parts, giving you four long, narrow rectangles.

Working on the long side, roll the dough up into a long, snake-like spiral, pinching the side seam shut to seal in the cinnamon and sugar and pinching both ends shut as well.

Braid each set of 4 on a greased jelly roll pan or cookie sheet into a round challah following the braiding instructions for the 4-strand, round challah braid. Cover with a clean kitchen towel and let dough rise for another 2 hours or so.

**Baking:**

Preheat your oven to 350 degrees (180 C). If you prefer your challahs glossy on the outside, make an egg wash by mixing 1 egg with a tbsp. (15 ml) of cold water. Brush the egg wash over the outside surface of the challah. Bake until the humps of the challah are golden brown and the crevices are starting to brown, and when the challah sounds hollow when you knock on it, which can take anywhere from ½ hour to 45 minutes depending on your oven

## Challah with Chocolate Tunnels (Pareve)

**Yeast preparation:**

½ cup water (120 ml) (110 degrees, or 40 degrees centigrade)
1 packet or 2 ½ tsp of yeast (13 ml)
1 tsp. sugar (5 ml)

Mix the water, sugar and yeast in the mixing bowl. Let sit for a few minutes to make sure the yeast is active and begins foaming, then proceed to dough preparation.

**Dough Preparation:**

1 cup water (225 ml)
1 egg
3 egg yolks
¾ cup honey (165 ml)
2 tbsp. vegetable oil (30 ml)
5-7 cups flour (1125-1575 ml)
2 tsp. salt (10 ml)
2 tsp. vanilla (10 ml)

Add water, egg and egg yolk, honey, and oil to the yeast mixture, along with 3 cups (675 ml) of flour. Mix using dough hooks until batter is smooth. Mix in salt and vanilla. Gradually add flour, ½ cup (120 ml) at a time, until dough is smooth and not sticky. Cover with a clean kitchen towel and place in a greased bowl in warm location and allow to rise for at least 3 hours, punching it down periodically.

**Chocolate Filling:**

For pareve challah, chop a pareve chocolate bar into chip-sized pieces, or use pareve chocolate chips. If you're not making pareve challah, you can use normal semi-sweet chocolate chips. You'll need about 12 ounces of chopped chocolate total to make a nice chocolate/bread balance.

**Braiding:**

The instructions below are for making two smaller round challahs, but the recipe works perfectly well for 1 large round, 2 small rectangular, or 1 large rectangular challah. If you prefer that it's easy to alter the number of braids and the way you braid them.

For 2 small, round challahs:

Split dough into 2 halves. One at a time, use a rolling pin to roll each half into a rectangle about 20-24" long (50-60 cm.), and 12" wide (30 cm.) Cut each rectangle into 4 equal parts lengthwise, so you have 4 sections about 20-24" long (50-60 cm.) and 3" wide (8 cm.). Divide the chocolate chips into eight even portions to allow one portion for each of the braids you'll be making. Spread the chips evenly along the center of each rectangle, then pull the sides of the rectangle up over the chocolate and pinch the dough together, creating dough tunnels full of chocolate.

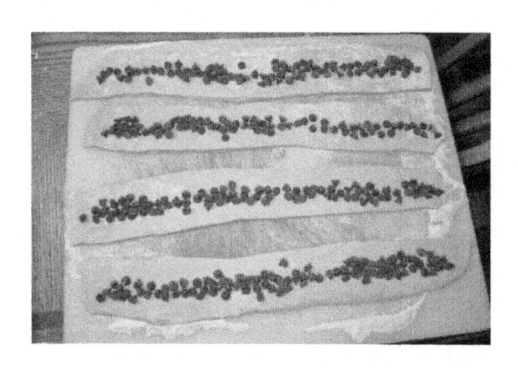

Pinch the ends together as well, sealing the chocolate in the dough. Braid each set of 4 on a greased jelly roll pan or cookie sheet into a round challah following the braiding instructions for the 4-strand, round challah braid. Cover with a clean kitchen towel and let dough rise for another 2 hours or so.

**Baking:**

Preheat your oven to 350 degrees (180 C). If you prefer your challahs glossy on the outside, make an egg wash by mixing 1 egg with one tbsp. (15 ml) of cold water. Brush the egg wash over the outside surface of the challah. Bake until the humps of the challah are golden brown and the crevices are starting to brown, and when the challah sounds hollow when you knock on it, which can take anywhere from ½ hour to 45 minutes depending on your oven

# Caramelized Onion Challah (Pareve)

A nice, savory challah that goes well with foods that would be complemented nicely by things with onions in them.

**Yeast preparation:**

½ cup water (120 ml) (110 degrees, or 40 degrees centigrade)
1 packet or 2 ½ tsp of yeast (13 ml)
1 tsp. sugar (5 ml)

Mix the water, sugar and yeast in the mixing bowl. Let sit for a few minutes to make sure the yeast is active and begins foaming, then proceed to dough preparation.

**Dough Preparation:**

1 cup water (225 ml)
3 eggs
¾ cup sugar (165 ml)
¾ cup vegetable oil (165 ml)
7-8 cups flour (1575-1800 ml)
1 tbsp. salt (15 ml)

Add water, eggs, sugar, and oil to the yeast mixture, along with 3 cups (675 ml) of flour. Mix using dough hooks until batter is smooth. Mix in salt. Gradually add flour, ½ cup (120 ml) at a time, until dough is smooth and not sticky. Cover with a clean kitchen towel and place in a greased bowl in warm location and allow to rise for at least 3 hours, punching it down periodically.

**Caramelized Onion Filling Preparation:**

2 tbsp.(30 ml) vegetable oil
2 large onions, sliced thinly

Fry onions in vegetable oil until they are golden brown in color (about 20 minutes, depending on skillet temperature. Cool.

**Braiding:**

The instructions below are for making two smaller rectangular challahs, but the recipe works perfectly well for 1 large round, 2 small round, or 1 large rectangular challah. If you prefer that it's easy to alter the number of braids and the way you braid them.

For 2 small, rectangular challahs:

Split dough into 2 parts. One at a time, use a rolling pin to roll each half into a rectangle about 20-24" long (50-60 cm.), and 12" wide (30 cm.)   Cut each rectangle into 3 equal parts lengthwise, so you have 3 sections about 20-24" long (50-60 cm.) and 4" wide (10 cm.). Divide the onions into six even portions to allow one portion for each of the braids you'll be making. Spread the onions evenly along the center of each rectangle of dough. Pull the sides of the dough up over the onions and pinch the dough together, creating dough tunnels full of onions.

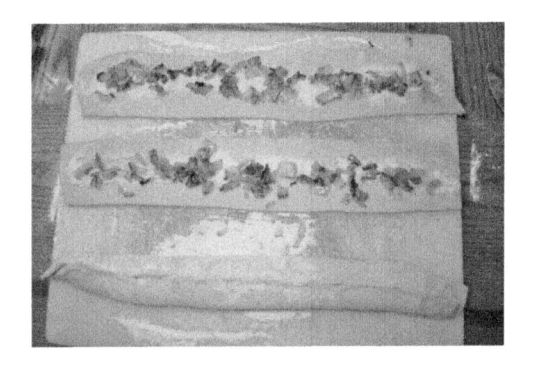

Pinch the ends together as well, sealing the onions in the dough. Braid each set of 3 on a greased jelly roll pan or cookie sheet into a rectangular challah following the braiding instructions for three-braid, rectangular challah. Cover with a clean kitchen towel and let dough rise for another 2 hours or so.

**Baking:**

Preheat your oven to 350 degrees (180 C).   If you prefer your challahs glossy on the outside, make an egg wash by mixing 1 egg with one tbsp. (15 ml) of cold water. Brush the egg wash over the outside surface of the challah. Bake until the humps of the challah are golden brown and the crevices are starting to brown, and when the challah sounds hollow when you knock on it, which can take anywhere from ½ hour to 45 minutes depending on your oven

# Caramelized Onion Challah with Parmesan (Dairy)

This is exactly the same as the previous recipe, except that it also includes the mellowness of parmesan cheese to complement the caramelized onions.

**Yeast preparation:**

½ cup water (120 ml) (110 degrees, or 40 degrees centigrade)
1 packet or 2 ½ tsp of yeast (13 ml)
1 tsp. sugar (5 ml)

Mix the water, sugar and yeast in the mixing bowl. Let sit for a few minutes to make sure the yeast is active and begins foaming, then proceed to dough preparation.

**Dough Preparation:**

1 cup water (225 ml)
3 eggs
¾ cup sugar (165 ml)
¾ cup vegetable oil (165 ml)
7-8 cups flour (1575-1800 ml)
1 tbsp. salt (15 ml)

Add water, eggs, sugar, and oil to the yeast mixture, along with 3 cups (675 ml) of flour. Mix using dough hooks until batter is smooth. Mix in salt. Gradually add flour, ½ cup (120 ml) at a time, until dough is smooth and not sticky. Cover with a clean kitchen towel and place in a greased bowl in warm location and allow to rise for at least 3 hours, punching it down periodically.

**Caramelized Onion Filling Preparation:**

2 tbsp. (30 ml) vegetable oil
2 large onions, sliced thinly

Fry onions in vegetable oil until they are golden brown in color (about 20 minutes, depending on skillet temperature. Cool.

**Braiding:**

1 cup grated parmesan cheese

The instructions below are for making two smaller rectangular challahs, but the recipe works perfectly well for 1 large round, 2 small round, or 1 large rectangular challah. If you prefer that it's easy to alter the number of braids and the way you braid them.

For 2 small, rectangular challahs:

Split dough into 2 parts. One at a time, use a rolling pin to roll each half into a rectangle about 20-24" long (50-60 cm.), and 12" wide (30 cm.)   Cut each rectangle into 3 equal parts lengthwise, so you have 3 sections about 20-24" long (50-60 cm.) and 4" wide (10 cm). Divide the fried onions and the parmesan cheese into six even portions to allow one portion for each of the braids you'll be making. Spread the onions evenly along the center of each rectangle, then spread the parmesan down each rectangle as well. Pull the sides of the rectangle up over the onions and pinch the dough together, creating dough tunnels full of onions and cheese. Pinch the ends together as well, sealing the onions and cheese in the dough. Braid each set of 3 onto a greased jelly roll pan or cookie sheet into a rectangular challah following the braiding instructions for three-braid, rectangular challah. Cover with a clean kitchen towel and let dough rise for another 2 hours or so.

**Baking:**

Preheat your oven to 350 degrees (180 C). If you prefer your challahs glossy on the outside, make an egg wash by mixing 1 egg with one tbsp. (15 ml) of cold water. Brush the egg wash over the outside surface of the challah. Bake until the humps of the challah are golden brown and the crevices are starting to brown, and when the challah sounds hollow when you knock on it, which can take anywhere from ½ hour to 45 minutes depending on your oven. As an alternative, you can remove the challah when the humps are just starting to brown and sprinkle parmesan cheese on the outside for decorative effect, then bake until golden brown as above.

# Jalapeño Cheese Challah (Dairy)

A challah with a bit of bite for when you want something a bit more exciting.

**Dough Ingredients:**

2 cups milk (450 ml)
1/3 cup sugar (75 ml)
7 tbsp. butter (80 ml)
2 packets or 5 tsp. yeast (25 ml)
3 eggs
1 egg yolk
2 tsp. salt (10 ml)
6-7 cups flour (1325-1575ml
5 jalapeño peppers
2 cups of sharp cheddar cheese, shredded (450 ml)

**Scalding the milk:**

Scalding of milk might seem like an unnecessary step to many, as milk is now so well pasteurized that killing bacteria in it prior to bread making sounds old-fashioned. But scalding of milk serves another purpose when we're baking bread. The whey in milk can interact with the gluten in bread and change the raising process and bread texture unless is partially broken down by heating).

In a small saucepan, bring the milk, sugar, and butter almost to a boil. Pour into the mixing bowl and allow to cool until under 110 degrees (under 40 degrees centigrade). Stir in yeast and allow to proof for 5 minutes to make sure the yeast is active and begins foaming.

**Dough Preparation:**

Add 3 cups of flour (675 ml) and the eggs and egg yolk to the mixture already in the mixing bowl. Mix using dough hooks until batter is smooth. Mix in salt. Gradually add flour, ½ cup at a time (120 ml), until dough is smooth and not sticky. Cover with a clean kitchen towel and place in a greased bowl in warm location and allow to rise for at least 3 hours, punching it down periodically.

**Jalapeño and Cheese Filling Preparation:**

Cut jalapeños lengthwise into two halves, removing centers and seeds. Slice each half crossways into thin slices.

**Braiding:**

The instructions below are for making two smaller rectangular challahs, but the recipe works perfectly well for 1 large round, 2 small round, or 1 large rectangular challah. If you prefer that it's easy to alter the number of braids and the way you braid them.

For 2 small, rectangular challahs:

Split dough into 2 parts. One at a time, use a rolling pin to roll each half into a rectangle about 20-24" long (50-60 cm.), and 12" wide (30 cm.)   Cut each rectangle into 3 equal parts lengthwise, so you have 3 sections about 20-24" long (50-60 cm.) and 4" wide (10 cm.). Divide the jalapeños and the cheese into six even portions to allow one portion for each of the braids you'll be making. Spread the jalapeños evenly along the center of each rectangle of dough, then spread cheese evenly along each one. Pull the sides of the rectangle up over the filling and pinch the dough together, creating dough tunnels full of jalapeños and cheese. Pinch the ends together as well, sealing the filling in the dough. Braid each set of 3 on a greased jelly roll pan or cookie sheet into a rectangular challah following the braiding instructions for three-braid, rectangular challah. Cover with a clean kitchen towel and let dough rise for another 2 hours or so.

**Baking:**

Preheat your oven to 350 degrees (180 C). If you prefer your challahs glossy on the outside, make an egg wash by mixing 1 egg with one tbsp. (15 ml) of cold water. Brush the egg wash over the outside surface of the challah. Bake until the humps of the challah are golden brown and the crevices are starting to brown, and when the challah sounds hollow when you knock on it, which can take anywhere from ½ hour to 45 minutes depending on your oven. If you wish to sprinkle cheese on the top for that special appearance, pull the challahs out when they're just starting to brown and sprinkle the cheese on top, then return them to the oven for the final minutes of baking. This prevents the cheese from burning, which it would do if you sprinkled the cheese on prior to the start of baking.

# Garlic and Herb Challah (Pareve or Dairy)

An excellent complement to salmon or meat meals(if pareve margarine is used. This one has no sugar other than the honey that is in it, and uses olive oil for that special flavor.

**Yeast preparation:**

½ cup water (120 ml) (110 degrees, or 40 degrees centigrade)
¼ cup honey (55 ml)
2 packets or 5 tsp of yeast (25 ml)

Mix the water, honey and yeast in the mixing bowl. Let sit for a few minutes to make sure the yeast is active and begins foaming, then proceed to dough preparation.

**Dough Preparation:**

1 ¼ cups water (270 ml)
4 eggs
½ cup olive oil (115 ml)
8-9 cups flour (1800-2025 ml)
1 tbsp. salt (15 ml)

4 or more cloves of minced garlic, or equal amounts of prepared minced garlic
1 tsp. crushed dried basil (5 ml)
1 tsp. crushed dried thyme (5 ml)
1 tsp. crushed dried rosemary (5 ml)

Add water, eggs, and olive oil to the yeast mixture, along with 3 cups of flour (675 ml). Mix using dough hooks until batter is smooth. Mix in salt, garlic, basil, thyme, and rosemary. Gradually add flour, ½ cup (120 ml) at a time, until dough is smooth and not sticky. Cover with a clean kitchen towel and place in a greased bowl in warm location and allow to rise for at least 3 hours, punching it down periodically.

**Braiding:**

The instructions below are for making two medium-sized rectangular challahs, but it also works for 2 medium-sized round challahs. If you prefer that it's easy to alter the number of braids and the way you braid them.

For 2 medium, rectangular challahs:

Split dough into 2 parts, and then split each part into three. Shape each part into a snake about 20-24" long (50-60 cm). Braid each set of 3 onto a greased jelly roll pan or cookie sheet into a rectangular challah following the braiding instructions for three-braid, rectangular challah. Cover with a clean kitchen towel and let dough rise for another 2 hours or so.

**Topping Preparation and Baking:**

3 tbsp. butter (45 ml) (or pareve margarine for pareve challah)

1 clove garlic, minced, or equivalent amounts of prepared minced garlic

1 tsp. crushed dried basil (5 ml)

1 tsp. crushed dried thyme (5 ml)

1 tsp. crushed dried rosemary (5 ml)

Preheat your oven to 350 degrees (180 C). Melt the butter or margarine and add the garlic, basil, rosemary, and thyme. Brush the butter and herb mixture over each braided challah. Bake until the humps of the challah are golden brown and the crevices are starting to brown, and when the challah sounds hollow when you knock on it, which can take anywhere from ½ hour to 45 minutes depending on your oven

## Challah with Raisins or Craisins (Dairy or Pareve)

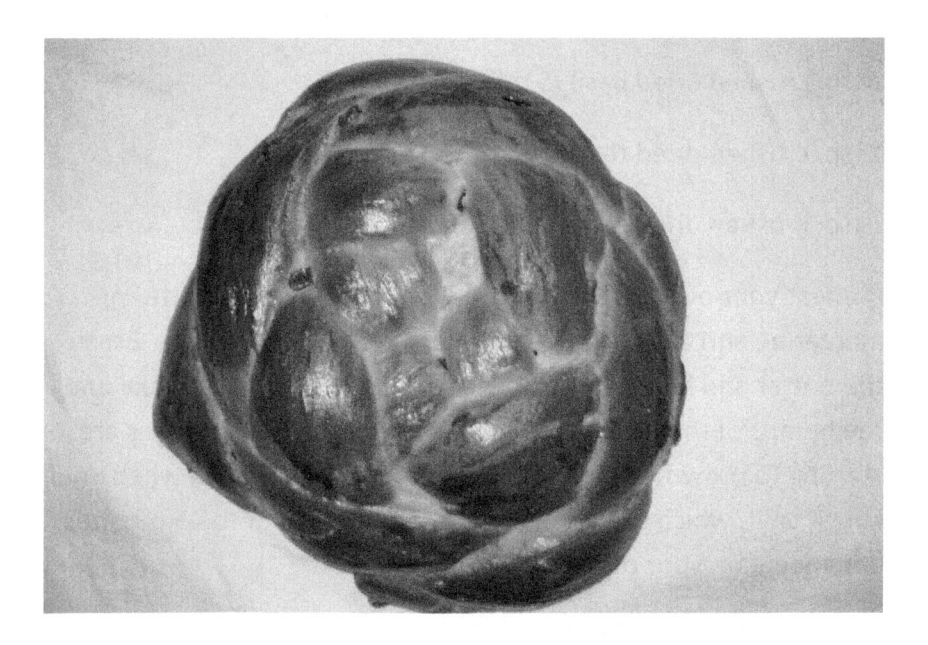

Personally, most of my family, myself included, think that putting raisins in a perfectly good challah is an abomination. But for those of you who like abominations, this is an excellent raisin challah. Alternatively, you can substitute equal quantities of craisins (dried cranberries) for the raisins (or you could substitute any other dried fruit, for that matter).

**Yeast preparation:**

½ cup water (120 ml) (110 degrees or 40 degrees centigrade)
2 packets or 5 tsp of yeast (25 ml)
1 tsp. sugar (5 ml)

Mix the water, sugar and yeast in the mixing bowl. Let sit for a few minutes to make sure the yeast is active and begins foaming, then proceed to dough preparation.

## The Complete and Simple Guide to Challah

**Dough Preparation:**

1 1/2 cups water (340 ml)
3 eggs
1/3 cup sugar (75 ml)
¾ cup honey (165 ml)
3/4 cup of softened butter (or pareve margarine if making pareve challah) (165 ml)
8-9 cups flour (1800-2025 ml)
1 tbsp. salt (15 ml)
1/8 tsp. nutmeg (1/2 -1 ml)
¼ tsp. cinnamon (1-1 ½ ml)
½ cup raisins (or craisins) (115 ml)

Soften the margarine or butter by leaving it out for several hours, or by microwaving it briefly. Add water, sugar, honey, butter, and eggs to yeast mixture, along with 3 cups (675 ml) of flour. Mix using dough hooks until batter is smooth. Mix in salt, nutmeg, and cinnamon. Gradually add flour, ½ cup (120 ml) at a time, until dough is smooth and not sticky. Add raisins gradually while mixing until they've evenly distributed through the dough. Cover with a clean kitchen towel and place in a greased bowl in warm location and allow to rise for at least 3 hours, punching it down periodically.

**Braiding:**

The instructions below are for making 2 medium-sized round challahs, but the recipe works perfectly well for 1 very large round, 2 medium-sized rectangular, or 1 very large rectangular challah. If you prefer that it's easy to alter the number of braids and the way you braid them.

2 medium-sized round challahs:

Split dough into 2 equal-sized parts, and then split each part into 4 equal parts. Using your hands, form each part into a snake about 20-24" long (50-60cm). Braid sets of four snakes together on a greased cookie sheet or jelly roll pan following the braiding instructions for 4-strand, round challah. Cover with a clean kitchen towel and let dough rise for another 2 hours or so.

**Baking:**

Preheat your oven to 350 degrees (180 C). If you prefer your challahs glossy on the outside, make an egg wash by mixing 1 egg with a tbsp. (15 ml) of cold water. Brush the egg wash over the outside surface of the challah. Likewise, if you like sesame seeds on your challah, you can sprinkle a tablespoon of sesame seeds across the top after brushing with the egg wash. Bake until the humps of the challah are golden brown and the crevices are starting to brown, and when the challah sounds hollow when you knock on it, which can take anywhere from ½ hour to 45 minutes depending on your oven

## Garlic Lovers' Challah (Pareve)

Cloves of garlic combined with minced garlic make this the bread for those who can't get enough of "the stinking rose" (as the Elizabethans referred to garlic).

### Garlic Preparation:

4 tbsp. minced garlic (60 ml)
1 tbsp. olive oil (15 ml)
4-10 cloves of garlic

Saute the minced garlic in olive oil until it starts to brown. Remove from the pan and let cool. Cut each garlic clove into 2-3 large pieces and sauté them until roasted and golden brown, adding more oil to the pan if necessary. Allow to cool.

### Yeast preparation:

½ cup water (120 ml) (110 degrees, or 40 degrees centigrade)
1 packet or 2 ½ tsp of yeast (13 ml)
1 tsp. sugar (5 ml)

Mix the water, sugar and yeast in the mixing bowl. Let sit for a few minutes to make sure the yeast is active and begins foaming, then proceed to dough preparation.

## Dough Preparation:

1 cup water (225 ml)
3 eggs
¾ cup sugar (165 ml)
¾ cup vegetable oil (165 ml)
8-9 cups flour (1800-2025 ml)
1 tbsp. salt (15 ml)

Add water, eggs, and oil to the yeast mixture, along with 3 cups (675 ml) of flour. Mix using dough hooks until batter is smooth. Mix in salt and then the sautéed minced garlic. Gradually add flour, ½ cup (120 ml) at a time, until dough is smooth and not sticky. In the final moments of mixing, add the garlic cloves and mix enough to spread them evenly through the dough. Cover with a clean kitchen towel and place in a greased bowl in warm location and allow to rise for at least 3 hours, punching it down periodically.

## Braiding:

The instructions below are for making two smaller rectangular challahs, but the recipe works perfectly well for 1 large round, 2 small round, or 1 large rectangular challah. If you prefer that it's easy to alter the number of braids and the way you braid them.

For 2 small, rectangular challahs:

Split dough into 2 parts, and then split each part into three. Shape each part out into a snake about 20-24" long (50-60cm). Braid each set of 3 onto a greased jelly roll pan or cookie sheet into a rectangular challah following the braiding instructions for three-braid, rectangular challah. Cover with a clean kitchen towel and let dough rise for another 2 hours or so.

**Baking:**

Preheat your oven to 350 degrees (180 C). If you prefer your challahs glossy on the outside, make an egg wash by mixing 1 egg with one tbsp. (15 ml) of cold water. Brush the egg wash over the outside surface of the challah. Bake until the humps of the challah are golden brown and the crevices are starting to brown, and when the challah sounds hollow when you knock on it, which can take anywhere from ½ hour to 45 minutes depending on your oven

# Cheese Challah (Dairy—Yeah, I know, that was obvious)

This is a great variant on the traditional challah recipe. Terrific for cheese lovers! Also, you can use actual butter in it because it's a dairy challah, and real butter just makes a challah that much more of a taste experience.

**Yeast preparation:**

½ cup water (120 ml) (110 degrees, or 40 degrees centigrade)
3 packets or 7 1/2 tsp of yeast (38 ml)
1 tsp. sugar (5 ml)

Mix the water, sugar and yeast in the mixing bowl. Let sit for a few minutes to make sure the yeast is active and begins foaming, then proceed to dough preparation.

**Dough Preparation:**

1 1/2 cups water (340 ml)
4 eggs
¼ cup brown sugar (55 ml)
¼ cup white sugar (55 ml)
½ cup of butter (120 ml)
7-8 cups flour (1575-1800 ml)

1 tbsp. salt (15 ml)

Soften the butter by leaving it out for several hours, or by microwaving it briefly. Add water, sugar, and egg to yeast mixture, along with 3 cups (675 ml) of flour. Mix using dough hooks until batter is smooth. Mix in salt. Gradually add flour, ½ cup (120 ml) at a time, until dough is smooth and not sticky. Cover with a clean kitchen towel and place in a greased bowl in warm location and allow to rise for at least 3 hours, punching it down periodically.

**Braiding:**

2-3 cups (450-657 ml) of grated sharp cheese, or more if you really like cheese

1 cup (225 ml) parmesan cheese

The instructions below are for making 2 smaller rectangular challahs, but the recipe works perfectly well for 1 large round, 2 small round, or 1 large rectangular challah. If you prefer that it's easy to alter the number of braids and the way you braid them.

For 2 small, rectangular challahs:

Split dough into 2 parts. One at a time, use a rolling pin to roll each half into a rectangle about 20-24" long (50-60 cm.), and 12" wide (30 cm.)   Cut each rectangle into 4 equal parts lengthwise, so you have 4 sections about 20-24" long (50-60 cm.) and 3" wide (8 cm.). Divide the grated and parmesan cheese into 6 equal portions. Spread the cheese along the center of each long, thin rectangle, then pull the sides of the rectangle up over the cheese and pinch the dough together, creating dough tunnels full of cheese. Pinch the ends together as well, sealing the cheese in the dough. Braid each set of 3 into a rectangular challah on a greased jelly roll pan or cookie sheet, following the braiding instructions for rectangular, three-braid challah. Cover with a clean kitchen towel and let dough rise for another 2 hours or so.

**Baking:**

Preheat your oven to 350 degrees (180 C). If you prefer your challahs glossy on the outside, make an egg wash by mixing 1 egg with one tbsp. (15 ml) of cold water. Brush the egg wash over the outside surface of the challah. Bake until the humps of the challah are golden brown and the crevices are starting to brown, and when the challah sounds hollow when you knock on it, which can take anywhere from ½ hour to 45 minutes depending on your oven. If you wish to sprinkle cheese on the top for that special appearance, pull the challahs out when they're just starting to brown and sprinkle the cheese on top, then return them to the oven for the final minutes of baking. This prevents the cheese from burning, which it would do if you sprinkled the cheese on prior to the start of baking.

# Salted Chocolate Challah (Dairy or Pareve)

This is another challah that's more dessert challah than main course challah, but it's great for chocolate lovers. Actually, that's damning with faint praise—it's absolutely perfect for chocolate lovers!

**Yeast preparation:**

½ cup water (120 ml) (110 degrees or 40 degrees centigrade)
2 packets or 5 tsp of yeast (25 ml)
1 tsp. sugar (5 ml)

Mix the water, sugar and yeast in the mixing bowl. Let sit for a few minutes to make sure the yeast is active and begins foaming, then proceed to dough preparation.

**Dough Preparation:**

1 1/2 cups water (340 ml)
3 eggs
2/3 cup sugar (150 ml)
1/3 cup vegetable oil (75 ml)
½ cup cocoa (120 ml)

7-8 cups flour (1575-1800 ml)
1 tbsp. salt (15 ml)
2 tsp. vanilla (10 ml)
2 cups chocolate chips or chopped pareve chocolate (450 ml)

Add water, sugar, oil, and eggs to yeast mixture, along with 3 cups(675 ml) of flour. Mix using dough hooks until batter is smooth. Mix in salt and vanilla. Gradually add flour, ½ cup (120 ml) at a time, until dough is smooth and not sticky. Add chocolate chips or chunks gradually while mixing until they've evenly distributed through the dough. Cover with a clean kitchen towel and place in a greased bowl in warm location and allow to rise for at least 3 hours, punching it down periodically.

**Braiding:**

The instructions below are for making 2 medium-sized round challahs, but the recipe works perfectly well for 1 very large round, 2 medium-sized rectangular, or 1 very large rectangular challah. If you prefer that it's easy to alter the number of braids and the way you braid them.

2 medium-sized round challahs:

Split dough into 2 equal-sized parts, and then split each part into 4 equal parts. Using your hands, form each part into a snake about 20-24" long (50-60cm). Braid sets of four snakes together on a greased cookie sheet or jelly roll pan following the braiding instructions for 4-strand, round challah. Cover with a clean kitchen towel and let dough rise for another 2 hours or so.

**Baking:**

Preheat your oven to 350 degrees (180 C).  Make an egg wash by mixing 1 egg with one tbsp. (15 ml) of cold water.  Brush the egg wash over the outside surface of the challah, then sprinkle with kosher salt.  Bake until the humps of the challah are dark brown and the crevices are starting to darken, and when the challah sounds hollow when you knock on it, which can take anywhere from ½ hour to 45 minutes depending on your oven

**Serving Suggestion:**

This one makes a great morning toast for the young ones, as well as the young at heart.

# Pesto Challah (Dairy)

This one gets its flavor from pesto. You can buy commercially prepared pesto, or, if you raise your own basil, prepare homemade pesto for the extra-fresh flavor.

**Yeast preparation:**

½ cup water  (120 ml) (110 degrees, or 40 degrees centigrade)
1 packet or 2 ½ tsp of yeast (38 ml)
1 tsp. sugar (5 ml)


Mix the water, sugar and yeast in the mixing bowl. Let sit for a few minutes to make sure the yeast is active and begins foaming, then proceed to dough preparation.

**Dough Preparation:**

1 cup water (225 ml)
3 eggs
¾ cup sugar (165 ml)
¾ cup vegetable oil (165 ml)
8-9 cups flour (1800-2025 ml)
6 tbsp. pesto (90 ml)
1 tbsp. salt (15 ml)

Add water, eggs, and oil to the yeast mixture, along with 3 cups (675 ml) of flour. Mix using dough hooks until batter is smooth. Mix in salt and then pesto. Gradually add flour, ½ cup (120 ml) at a time, until dough is smooth and not sticky. Cover with a clean kitchen towel and place in a greased bowl in warm location and allow to rise for at least 3 hours, punching it down periodically.

## Braiding:

The instructions below are for making two smaller rectangular challahs, but the recipe works perfectly well for 1 large round, 2 small round, or 1 large rectangular challah. If you prefer that it's easy to alter the number of braids and the way you braid them.

For 2 small, rectangular challahs:

Split dough into 2 parts, and then split each part into three. Shape each part out into a snake about 20-24" long (50-60cm). Braid each set of 3 onto a greased jelly roll pan or cookie sheet into a rectangular challah following the braiding instructions for three-braid, rectangular challah. Cover with a clean kitchen towel and let dough rise for another 2 hours or so.

## Baking:

Preheat your oven to 350 degrees (180 C). If you prefer your challahs glossy on the outside, make an egg wash by mixing 1 egg with one tbsp. (15 ml) of cold water. Brush the egg wash over the outside surface of the challah. Bake until the humps of the challah are golden brown and the crevices are starting to brown, and when the challah sounds hollow when you knock on it, which can take anywhere from ½ hour to 45 minutes depending on your oven

# Traditional Croissants (Dairy)

Okay, I know I can't pass croissants off as a challah recipe, not even if one thinks of them as very flaky, buttery, mini-challahs. But croissants are very fun to make, if a bit labor intensive, and the results are highly gratifying as well as a great way to impress your relatives and friends. They're also easier to make than most people realize, and fresh croissants are absolutely amazing to eat.

## Dough Preparation (makes 24-30 croissants)

2 packages or 5 tsp. yeast (25 ml)
1 ¼ cup of water (280 ml)
1 ¼ cup of milk (280 ml) (milk is not scalded because we're not trying to encourage formation of gluten when making croissants)
¾ cup of sugar (165 ml)
6 tbsp. of softened, unsalted butter (90 ml)
8 cups of flour (1800 ml)
1 ½ tbsp. of salt (23 ml)

Add liquid ingredients, yeast, sugar, and butter to mixing bowl along with 3 cups (675 ml) of flour. Mix together until blended, then add salt.  Next, add additional flour, half a cup (120 ml) at a time, until dough is smooth and not sticky.  Split the dough into two equal portions and flatten each portion into a round disk about 10 inches (25 cm) across.  Place each disk on a pie plate or dinner plate, wrap each with plastic to keep it from drying out, and refrigerate overnight.

**Layering and Rolling:  Butter preparation**

The following day, start by preparing the butter layer.  You'll need 2/3 of a pound (300 grams) of unsalted butter for each portion of dough, or 1 1/3 pound (600 grams) of unsalted butter total.  Each 2/3 pound (300 gram) portion should be cut into ½ inch (12 mm) wide slabs.  Make a square of the slabs on waxed paper (your square will be about 6 inches (15 cm) in each dimension).  Then place a piece of waxed paper on the top of the square and pound the butter square with your rolling pin until it softens and the separate slabs join together into one square.  Roll the square until it is a bit more than 7 ½ inches (about 19 cm) in both dimensions.

Neatly trim the sides down make a 7 ½ inch-square (19 cm-square) of butter, and put the trimmings on top of the slab, gently pressing the trimmings into the square without making the square any wider.  Refrigerate this butter portion and follow the same steps to make the second butter portion, which should also be refrigerated.

**Layering and Rolling: Dough Preparation**

Unwrap one of the disks of refrigerated dough and place it on a floured, large cutting board or other flat working surface. Roll it into a 10 ½ inch (27 cm) square. The dough will be stiff and fight you a bit, but keep pressing and pulling until you have a reasonably neat, even square 10 ½ inches (27 cm) on a side.

Retrieve one of the butter portions that you prepared earlier from the refrigerator and place it on the dough portion with the butter square oriented 45 degrees relative to the dough, so that the points of the butter are centered on the sides of the dough.

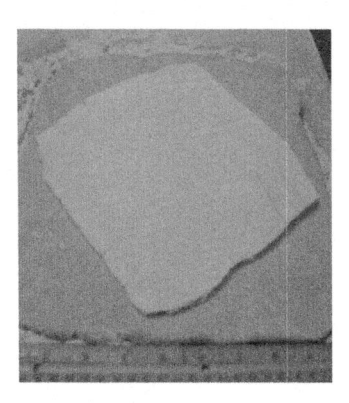

Fold the triangles of dough that are still uncovered over the butter, sealing the edges so the butter is completely sealed into the dough.

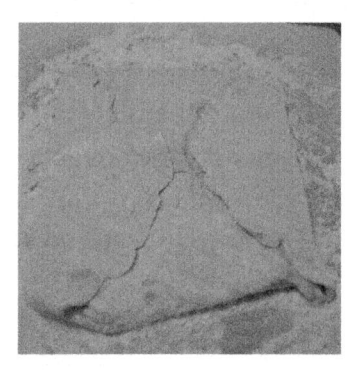

Once the dough is sealed over the butter on top, start rolling the dough lengthwise, concentrating on making it longer but not wider.  You want to roll the dough until you have a rectangle about 8 inches (20 cm) by 24 inches (60 cm), so keep working the dough longer and longer until you get to those dimensions.  The dough will get easier to work as you go along, but it will tend to spring back as you roll, so you have to be patient and stretch it out as you go.

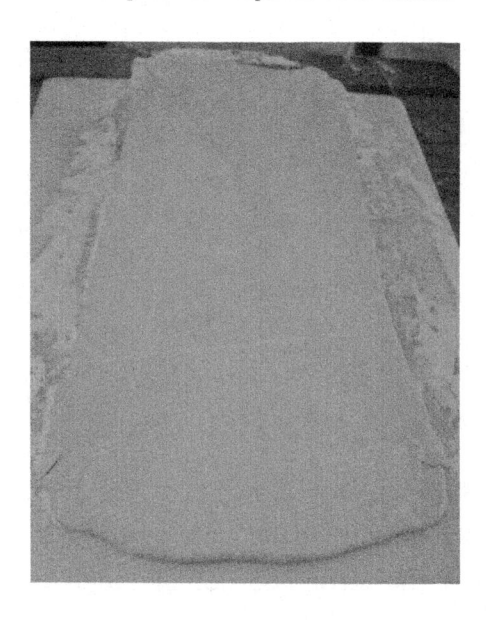

Once you have the dough in a rectangle that is 8 by 24 inches (20 by 60 cm), fold one third of the dough up until it covers the middle third, leaving the top third uncovered.

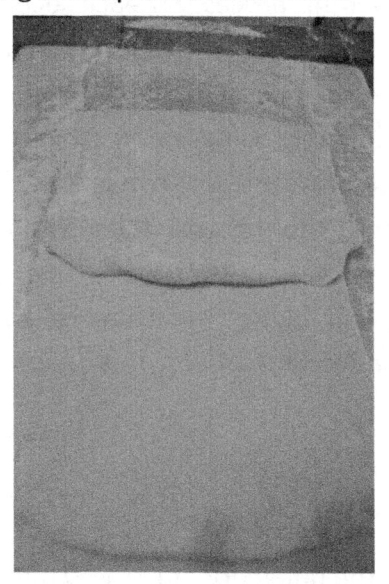

Brush off any flour adhering to the dough you just folded, then fold the remaining third down over the other, already folded section, and brush the flour off of the top of that section.

Place the now three-layered, 8 inch by 8 inch (20 cm by 20 cm) portion of dough back on the pie plate or dish and refrigerate it while you prepare the second portion of dough in the same fashion.

Once both sections of dough have undergone their first folding, you'll need to repeat this process for each section 2 more times. Rotate the dough 90 degrees for the second rolling, so that the seams that were on the sides in the first rolling are now at the ends, roll the dough until you have a rectangle 8 inches by 24 inches (20 by 60 cm), fold the dough over into thirds again, and refrigerate it while you do the same thing with the second portion.  Then repeat the whole process a third time.  At the end of the third rolling and folding, you'll have an amazing 28 very thin layers of dough sandwiching 27 very thin layers of butter.


Final Rolling and Cutting:

After refrigerating the dough for at least 30 minutes, take the first portion and begin rolling it out again on a floured surface.  This time, though, you're going to be rolling the dough out to a rectangle that is 8 inches (20 cm) wide and 44 inches (110 cm) long.  This takes a **lot** of rolling!  You have to work and work the dough, first one end, then the middle, then the other end, going back and forth and stretching the dough with your hands in between to help the process along.  Be careful, though—the layers of butter and dough are very, very thin.  It's possible you'll have trouble getting to 44 inches (110 cm) in length.  If it becomes extraordinarily difficult to go much past 33 inches (90 cm), you can stop at that point, but the croissants will be larger and thicker if that is the case.  If the dough starts getting sticky at this point you can lightly add some flour to it.

Once you have finished rolling, it's time for measuring and cutting.  Using a yardstick or meter stick, make a small cut in the dough every 5 inches (12.5 cm), starting from one end and working your way to the other.

Move the yardstick to the other side of the dough, and do the same thing, but make sure these marks start 2 ½ inches (6.25 cm) offset from the ones at the other side, so that each mark on the opposite side is half-way in between two marks from the other side.

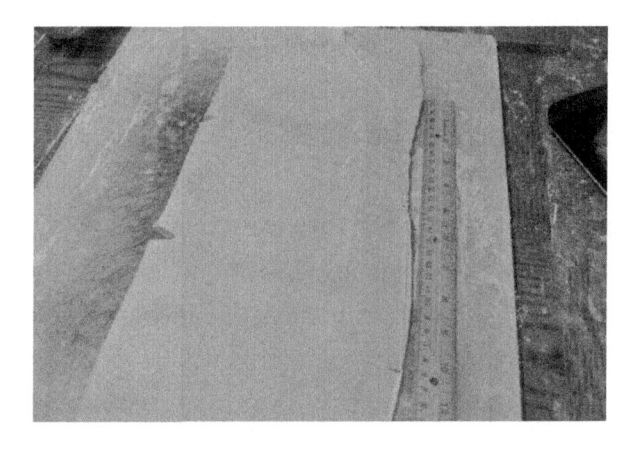

Now you can begin cutting triangles by cutting diagonally from the first mark on one side of the dough to the first mark on the other side. Proceed up the dough, cutting each triangle off.

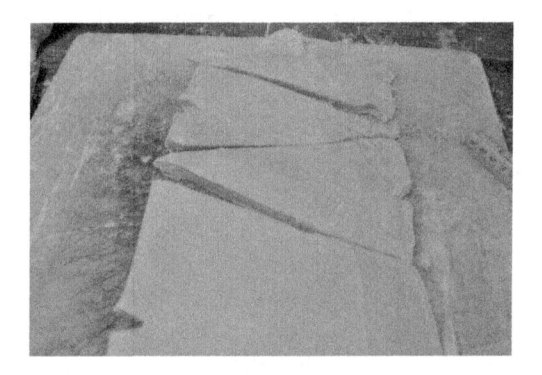

You'll end up with 12-15 croissants, depending on whether you were able to roll the dough out to full length or not.

Make a small cut about ½ inch (12 mm) long in the center of the short side of each triangle. This will allow you to pull that side slightly apart creating a notch on the short side.

Placing a hand on either side of the notch, begin rolling the croissant up, ending at the pointed end.

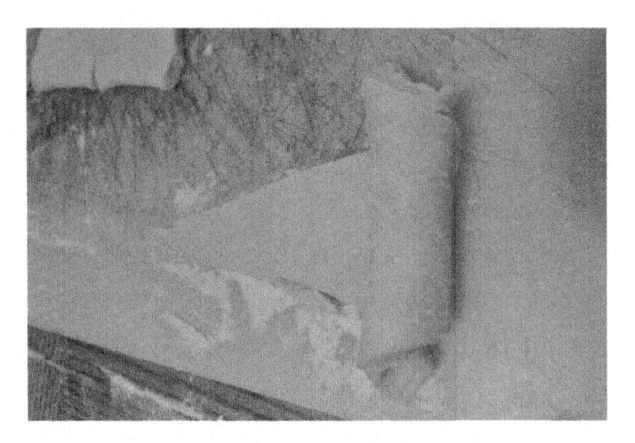

Curve the rolled croissant slightly so the ears come together—you can even allow them to touch if you wish. Place each croissant on a baking sheet to rise, leaving space between them because they will rise considerably over the next few hours.

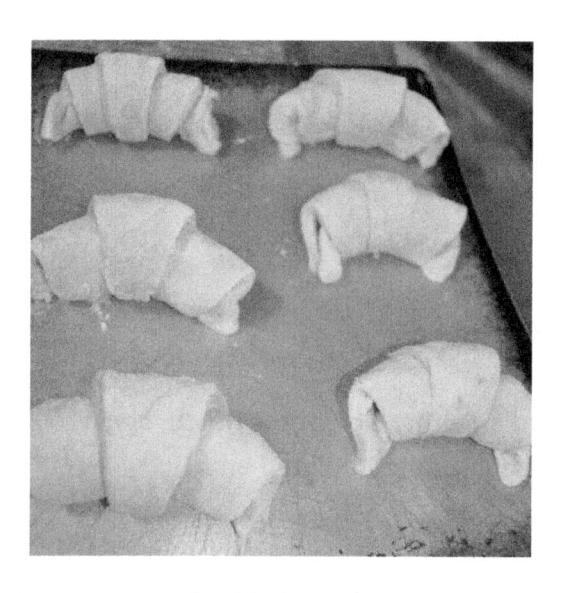

I usually put six on a standard baking sheet. It is best to use baking sheets with edges if possible, to prevent butter leaking from the croissants burning on the bottom of the oven. If using flat baking sheets, it is best to put another pan under the baking croissants to catch any leaking butter. Prepare an egg wash by taking an egg and beating it with one tbsp.. (15 ml) of cold water until well blended. Brush each croissant with the egg wash, coating each exposed surface so that the croissants won't dry out during the raising process. Save leftover egg wash in the refrigerator—you'll need it again just before baking. There is no need to cover the croissants while they're rising.

After allowing the croissants to rise for several hours, preheat an oven to 400 degrees. Brush the croissants with the egg wash a second time and bake them for about 20 minutes, or until they're golden brown. (Baking times may vary due to variations in croissant sizes.) Allow the croissants to cool before removing from the baking sheets.

**Variations:**

One of the best variants on this recipe is to make filled croissants. One can make cheese croissants, for example, by putting a quantity of grated cheese just under the notch before you start rolling, and then rolling the cheese into the dough as you roll the croissant up. What I'd recommend, though, is chocolate filled croissants. Place a large quantity of chocolate chips just under the notch prior to rolling each croissant and roll those chips into the dough. The results are highly recommended.

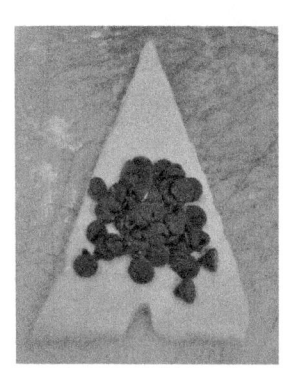

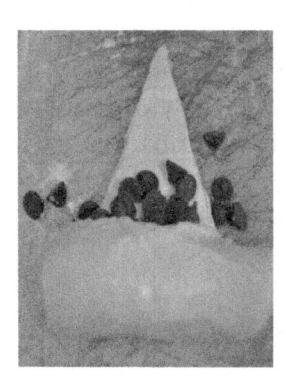

# Pita (Pareve)

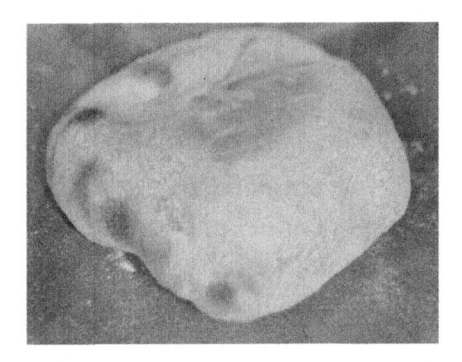

Pita is also not challah, but it is at least Middle Eastern. It's also delicious, especially with homemade hummus, and it's childishly simple to make, and quick to bake too!

**Dough preparation:**

1 cup water (225 ml) (110 degrees, or 40 degrees centigrade)
1 tsp. sugar (5 ml)
1 packet or 2 ½ tsp of yeast (13 ml)
3 cups flour, more or less (675 ml)
2 tsp. salt (10 ml)
2 tsp. olive oil (10 ml)

Mix the water, sugar and yeast in the mixing bowl. Let sit for a few minutes to make sure the yeast is active and begins foaming, then proceed to dough preparation.

Using dough hooks, add 1 cup (225 ml) of flour to the yeast and sugar mixture and mix until smooth. Add the salt and the olive oil. Gradually add the remaining flour, ½ cup (120 ml) at a time, until the dough is smooth and not sticky. Place in a greased bowl in a warm location and cover with a clean kitchen towel and allow to rise for at least 2 hours.

## Preparation and Baking:

From the main mass of dough, pull off small lumps of dough measuring about 2-3 inches (5-7.5 cm) across and roll them into balls. Place each ball on a floured cutting board and roll the dough out into a circle less than a quarter of an inch (60 mm) thick, which should result in a disk about 5-6 inches (12-15 cm) wide. Arrange several disks on a baking sheet.

Set your oven on "Broil" and bake for between 3 and 5 minutes, depending on the heat of your broiler, watching continuously for the tops to start to brown. The disks may puff up during this process, but don't worry about that, they'll collapse again when removed from the oven.

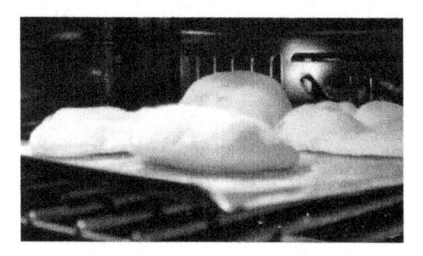

Once the tops start to brown, slide the baking sheet out and flip the disks over, then put them back in and bake for a few more minutes, until the second side starts to brown. Remove and allow to cool enough to eat, then serve immediately, preferably with homemade hummus.

# Farmhouse Cinnamon Rolls (Dairy) (Adapted from the <u>Kitchen Klatter</u> Cookbook)

Even though cinnamon rolls aren't challah, they played a prominent role in my interest in bread baking. As I mentioned in opening this recipe book, my whole adventure with challah began with the cinnamon rolls of the farmhouse of my childhood. Here is the latest variation on the cinnamon roll recipe I learned from my mother.

**Dough preparation:**

1/2 cup water (120 ml) (110 degrees, or 40 degrees centigrade)
1 tbsp. sugar (15 ml)
2 packets or 5 tsp. of yeast (25 ml)

Mix the water, sugar and yeast in the mixing bowl. Let sit for a few minutes to make sure the yeast is active and begins foaming, then proceed to dough preparation.

2 cups warm water (450 ml)(110 degrees, or 40 degrees centigrade)

½ cup sugar (120 ml)

3 eggs

½ cup butter, softened (120 ml)

2 tsp. salt (10 ml)

8 cups flour, more or less (1800 ml)

Using dough hooks, add 3 cups (675 ml) of flour to the yeast and sugar mixture, along with the additional water, the sugar, the eggs, the salt, and the softened butter, and mix until well blended. Gradually add the remaining flour, ½ cup (120 ml) at a time, until the dough is smooth and not sticky. Place in a greased bowl in warm location and cover with a clean kitchen towel and allow to rise for at least 2 hours.

**Preparation and Baking:**

You'll need about ½ cup (120 ml) of softened butter, 1 cup (225 ml) sugar, and several tbsp. (50 ml or more) of cinnamon for this step.

Separate the dough into two equal sized sections, so you can work on one section at a time. Roll one section of the dough out into a rectangle roughly 20 in. by 24 in. (50cm by 60 cm). The dough should end up less than ¼ in. (1/3 cm.) thick at this point. Make a faint line down the middle of the dough, and spread the right half of the dough with a thin layer of softened butter. Sprinkle sugar in an even layer over the butter, then sprinkle cinnamon on top of the sugar. (Don't be afraid to go heavy on the cinnamon and sugar. The dough will rise, and the layers will get much thicker than they are now.)

Carefully fold the uncovered left side of the dough across the cinnamon and sugar side, covering the cinnamon and sugar completely. Turn the dough 90 degrees on the cutting board and roll it out again to 20 in. by 24 in. (50cm by 60 cm). Repeat the previous steps of marking the center of the dough and spreading the right half with butter, cinnamon, and sugar. Fold the left half across the right once again. Rotate the dough 90 degrees and repeat this entire process one more time, rolling, applying cinnamon and sugar to half the dough, and folding the other half over. Turn the dough 90 degrees again, and roll it out to about 20 in. by 24 in. (50cm by 60 cm). Using a sharp knife, slice the dough into strips about 2 inches wide. Starting on one end, roll the strips up into spirals and place them side-by-side into a greased cake pan.

You can get about 8 spiral rolls in a 9 inch by 13 inch cake pan (23 cm X 31 cm). This recipe makes between 12 and 15 such rolls, so you'll need a second small pan to hold the entire recipe.

Cover the prepared rolls in their pans and allow them to rise for 2-3 hours.

Preheat your oven to 350 degrees (180 centigrade). Bake for about 45 minutes (baking time will vary enormously depending on the size of your pans, the thickness of your rolls, and the qualities of your oven. The rolls should be golden brown on top when done.

Powdered Sugar Icing:

2 cups (450 ml) powdered sugar

1 tsp. (5 ml) vanilla or almond flavoring

Milk or cream

Measure the powdered sugar into a small bowl. Slowly stir in milk or cream until a thick icing has been created, adding the vanilla at the end. Spread liberally over the tops of the baked cinnamon rolls.

# Onion Bialys (Pareve)

I'm going to close this volume with a traditional Jewish favorite. Onion Bialys. Bialys are the slightly lighter cousin of bagels, and have a filling in the center instead of a hole. Bialys are quick and easy to make, and so delicious fresh from the oven!

**Filling Preparation:**

2 tbsp. (30 ml) dry onion flakes
2 tsp. (10 ml) poppy seeds
1 tbsp. (15 ml) vegetable oil

Place the onion flakes in a small bowl and add water to cover. Allow the onion flakes to soak until they soak up enough moisture to be the consistency of fresh onions. Pat dry with a paper towel. Add the oil and poppy seeds and mix thoroughly, then set aside for later use.

**Dough preparation:**

1 ¾ cup water (350 ml) (110 degrees, or 40 degrees centigrade)
1 packet or 2 ½ tsp of yeast (13 ml)
5 tsp. sugar (25 ml)
2 tsp. salt (10 ml)
4-6 cups of flour (900-1200 ml)

Add the water, yeast, and sugar to the mixing bowl and beat until the yeast is dissolved.  Using dough hooks, add 1 cup (225 ml) of flour to the yeast and sugar mixture and mix until smooth. Add the salt. Gradually add the remaining flour, ½ cup (120 ml) at a time, until the dough is smooth and not sticky. Cover with a clean kitchen towel and place in a greased bowl in warm location and allow to rise for at about  2 hours, punching the dough down after the first hour.

**Preparation and Baking:**

Divide the dough into 24 equally-sized parts, and roll each part into a ball. Allow the dough to rest for 15 minutes. Either dust cookie sheets with corn meal or grease the cookie sheets. Flatten each ball into a disk about 4 inches (10 cm) wide. Allow to rise for 30 minutes. Next, create a depression in the center of each disk. Divide the onion and poppy seed mixture into 24 portions and place a portion into each depression. Let the finished bialys rise for another 20 minutes. Preheat your oven to 425 degrees (218 degrees centigrade).  Bake bialys for 15 to 20 minutes, until they are starting to brown on the tops.

For best enjoyment, serve immediately.  Bialys can be sliced like bagels and covered with lox, tomato, onion, and cream cheese, can be used as the basis for sandwiches, or can simply be enjoyed as a breakfast or dinner roll.

**A Closing Message:**

And there  you have it. Twenty of my favorite recipes, all in one slim, reasonably priced volume. I hope you and your own families enjoy making and eating these as much as our extended family has!

## ABOUT THE AUTHOR

Dr. Dean Richards grew up on a dairy farm near Columbus Junction, Iowa. Finding himself not fond of cold, damp winters and hot, humid summers working among piles of manure, he studied psychology at the University of Iowa and then got his Ph. D. in the subject from Carnegie-Mellon University. Upon graduation he left cows behind forever and moved to Los Angeles. After marrying his lovely wife, Dr. Andrea Richards, they raised three perfectly lovely children, one of whom is pursuing rabbinical studies and whose need for fresh challah each week inspired the production of this volume. When he's not baking, Dr. Richards teaches psychology online and onsite for a number of universities. In addition to this book of recipes, he is the author of two popular books in psychology written for professionals and nonprofessionals as well, *Psychology in Plain English* and *More Psychology in Plain English*. Both this volume and the two of them are available in paperback and for Kindle and Kindle Reader Apps on Amazon.com.

Dean enjoys hearing from readers, and appreciates online reviewers. If you'd like to contact him, you can do so at this email address:

deanrichardsbooks@gmail.com

Reviews can be posted for this volume on its web page on Amazon.com. The Amazon Kindle app for smartphones, tablets, and desktop computers can also be downloaded from Amazon.com. If you liked this book, please recommend it to a friend, or order a copy through Amazon to give as a lovely gift! Heck, order 10 and give them to friends and relatives—shipping costs are much cheaper if you do!

Made in the USA
Middletown, DE
14 November 2020